Rusty and Roo
take a tumble

By Kathy Carter

Illustrated by Faye Hobson

*For those cheeky equines,
Rumba, Humbug and Badger.*

Copyright 2016 Kathy Carter & Faye Hobson.

The rights of Kathy Carter to be identified as the author, and of Faye Hobson to be identified as the illustrator of this work, have been asserted by them in accordance with the Copyright, Designs and Patents Act 1998.

All rights reserved. No part of this publication may be reproduced, stored in or introduced into a retrieval system, or transmitted in any form, or by any means (electronic, mechanical, photocopying, recording or otherwise), without prior permission of the author. Any person who does any unauthorized act in relation to this publication may be liable to criminal prosecution and civil claims for damages.

First Published in 2016 by Sirenia Books. A division of Sirenia Ltd.
www.sireniabooks.com

ISBN: 978-0-9934392-4-7
A CIP catalogue record is available for this book from the British Library.

Cover design and page layout by Lighthouse24.

*Rusty and Roo are here for you
   with a whinny, bray, clip clop.
Meet their friends and see why
   their adventures never stop.*

*Rusty the pony leads the herd,
   donkey Roo is at his side.
Just another day of fun
   at Popples' Ranch and Ride.*

Rusty and Roo
take a tumble

Rusty and Roo are best of friends,
   we see them side-by-side.
The fun with them, it never ends,
   at Popples' Ranch and Ride.

Rusty thinks he's ten feet tall,
   the pony leads the herd.
Roo the donkey likes to bray,
   the loudest we have heard.

At Mrs Popples' Ranch and Ride,
adventures never stop.
Rusty and Roo will save the day
with a whinny, bray, clip clop.

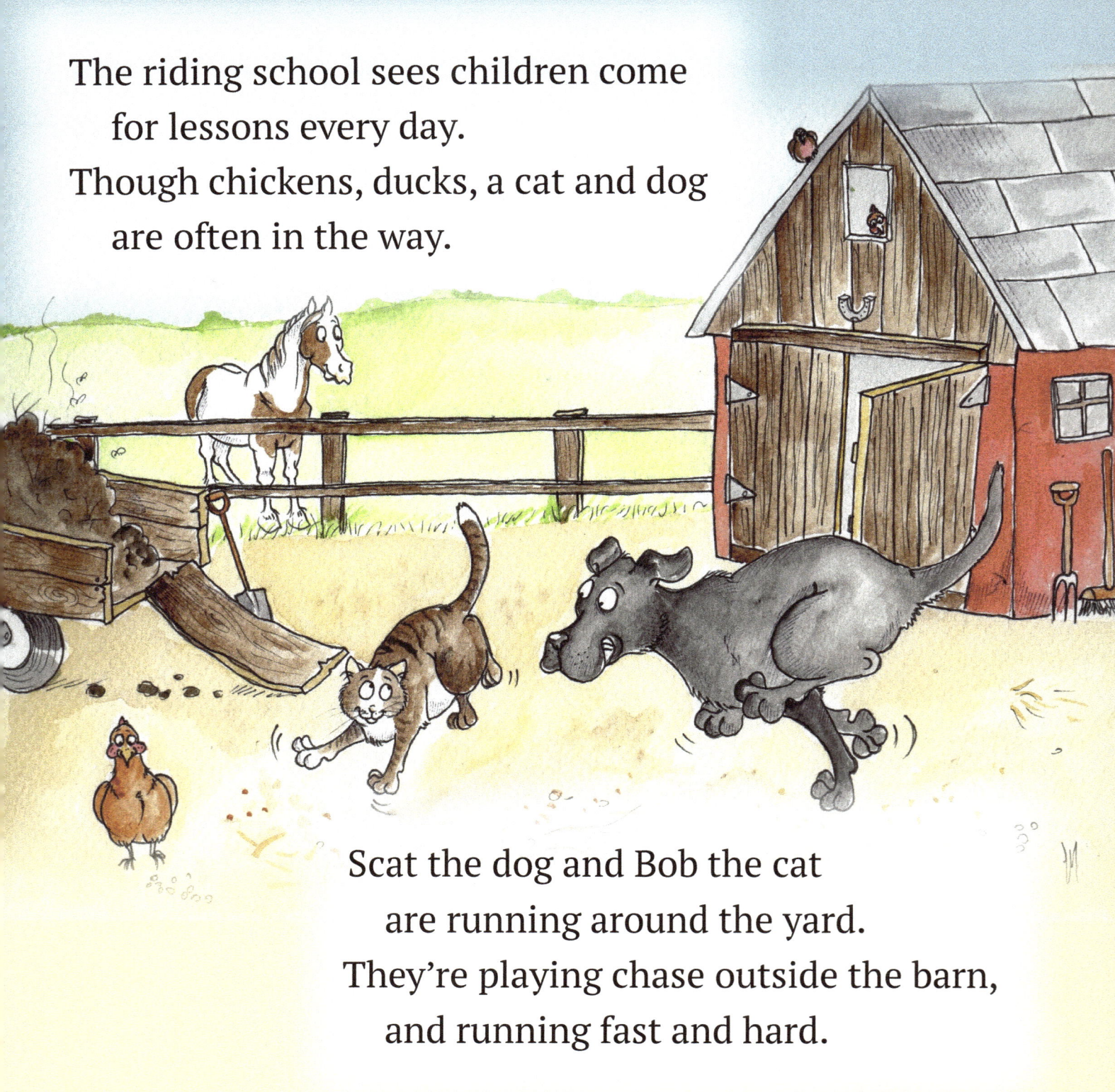

The riding school sees children come
for lessons every day.
Though chickens, ducks, a cat and dog
are often in the way.

Scat the dog and Bob the cat
are running around the yard.
They're playing chase outside the barn,
and running fast and hard.

Bob climbs the ramp, he's in the muck,
we hear a squelchy plop.

Rusty and Roo will save the day
with a whinny, bray, clip clop.

The friends are hearing all the noise
    and come to rescue Bob.
Scat will surely try to help –
    where is that naughty dog?

Roo trots up the little ramp
    to rescue Bob, who's stuck.
But he trips and takes a tumble
    in the very mucky muck.

Rusty rolls his eyes and shakes his little pony head.
"Scat and Bob, you shouldn't play here, Mrs Popples said."

Rusty climbs the ramp and grabs
the tail of donkey, Roo.
The donkey reaches for the cat
and holds his tail too.

Scat the dog joins in to help,
and pulls with all his might.
Little Buck, a helpful duck,
joins in this silly sight.

They pull and pull and then a splosh,
   as Bob and Roo are free.
The friends are drenched in mucky muck –
   a funny sight to see.

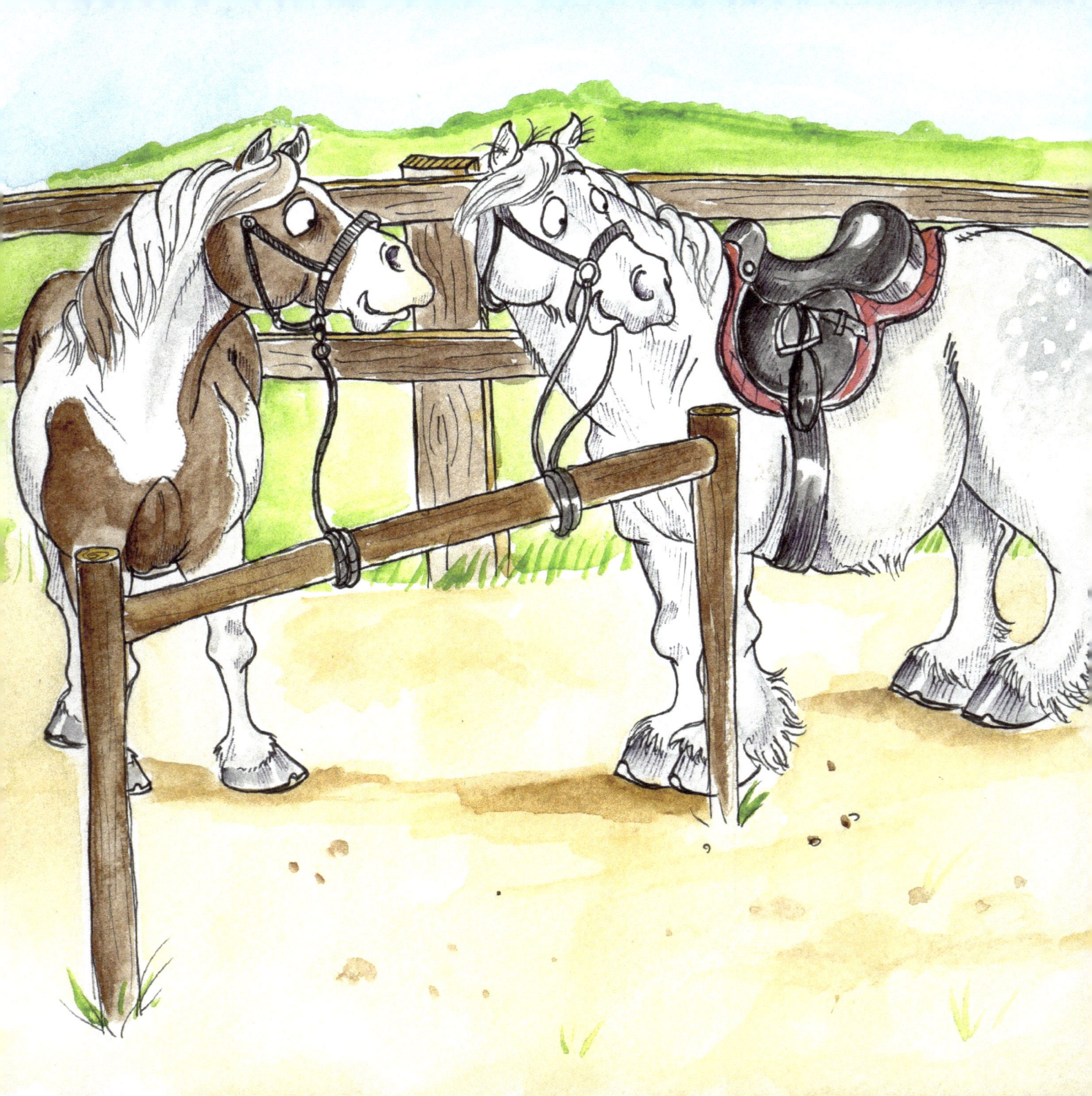

Mrs Popples marches in
  with Badger, a grey cob.
"Come on you silly animals,
  we are here to do a job.
It's time for lessons now,
  the children want to learn to ride.
Why don't you have a tidy up
  and go and play outside?"

Mrs Popples leads two horses
out into the ring.
Badger with his dappled rump
and Merlin with his bling.

The children mount the horses,
then canter, walk and trot.
Badger sees a tasty hedge.
He likes to eat. A lot.

He canters off, the hedge in sight,
and ducks beneath the rail.
The rider is now left behind –
the boy begins to wail.

Mrs Popples shakes her fist
and has an angry hop.
Rusty and Roo will save the day
with a whinny, bray, clip clop.

Roo trots up before
    the little boy can hit the deck.
"It's alright – hold my flappy ears
    and then slide down my neck."

The child is safe and happy,
    Roo and Rusty at his side.
Just another day of fun
    at Popples' Ranch and Ride.

THE END

Sirenia Books is committed to providing beautiful, enchanting books that will become firm favourites with children, carers, educators and families alike.

The Rusty and Roo series is available as a paperback from online retailers worldwide. Alternatively, please ask your local bricks and mortar book-store or equestrian outlet to order you a copy from their usual book distributor.

Other titles available:
Alfie's Magic Hat: Fun At The Zoo
Alfie's Magic Hat: Fun At The Zoo - Colouring Book
Rusty and Roo Take A Tumble - Colouring Book

Coming soon:
Alfie's Magic Hat: Farmyard Fun
Rusty and Roo Solve A Mystery

www.sireniabooks.com

www.ingramcontent.com/pod-product-compliance
Lightning Source LLC
Chambersburg PA
CBHW061932290426
44113CB00024B/2891